GW00694226

RECALLING LONDON EAST

To Peter who paddles his own canoe

Recalling London East

poems by

Pat Francis

illustrations by

Jane Colling

Paekakariki Press

2020

This is number 93
of an edition of 250 copies.

Poems © 2020, Pat Francis

Images © 2020, Jane Colling
janecolling.co.uk

Text set in 12pt 'Monotype' Garamond 156
by Paekakariki Press.

Isbn: 978-1908133-41-0

Printed at Paekakariki Press,
Walthamstow
paekakarikipress.com

Contents

Some Londoners

Family Story

Nobody of note
in my family
not even a chorister
or town councillor.

I never heard one went
to church or chapel
addressed a crowd
of protesters or joined

a party. Their only
pulse of life beyond
keeping going was
song and dance

practised strictly in the
parlour, not the pub.
They savoured words,
but literature was distant.

'How d'you spell…?'
my mother would ask,
she writing letters,
me at my homework.

Before I could answer:
'Never mind', she said,
I've put something else'.
She made no mistakes.

And my grandmother,
schooled for a while
for a few pennies a week,
wrote rhythmic letters:

'Dear Pat' each brief
sentence began, like
a refrain. No errors.
I never saw her read.

Back a generation,
some signed, some
made their mark
as they recorded

lives and deaths,
names and dates.
They left no word
of pain or pleasure.

This is a late posy
for all that hidden
life, for all those
silent singers.

Autumn, London 1950s

in memory of my mother

Season of dank yellow fog, dark streets
and a cold wait at the bus-stop;
pears yellow-ripe
in the greengrocer's window
fragrant and heavy in the bowl at home;
how could she resist?

Catching juice as it ran down her chin
perhaps, she thought, just this once
I might—but no.
She caught each painful breath,
wheezing, as her lungs refused
what her tongue had relished.

Such punishment
for so innocent a temptation.

High Church

1940s

Father Evans left the challenge of
Africa for the challenge of
Plaistow: a pitifully tiny
congregation, nobody to play
hymns, shy singing from
embarrassed women—only
women—in the pews.

Little girls went to Sunday School
so Mum and Dad could snooze,
oblivious to ritual. St Martins
was Anglo-Catholic because
Plaistow was close to Essex
where Conrad Noel had
once preached revolution.

Noel, the Red Vicar, had flown
the green flag of Sinn Fein and
the red flag of Socialism side
by side in his Thaxted church,
drawing in the politically daring,
luring the indifferent with joyful
inflammatory Christian Socialism.

Aunt Min

My thin-lipped aunt loved me
as much as her heart would allow.
The giggly aunts were easier
to love, though Aunt Min
had a dog we took for walks.

Sweets were to be sucked
not crunched; but once
she bought me a peach
that glowed, scented gold,
a marvel in my hand.

Aunt Min sang in a reedy
refined voice, told stories
about little princesses. I
listened carefully knowing
she meant to please.

She did her best for years
poor Aunt Min, until asked
to break the news and spare
my mother's feelings.
Her courage failed her.

'Is he dead?' I had to ask
her averted face. I was hustled
home on a bus, my throat locked
against the tears she dreaded.
Some failures are hard to forgive.

Uncle Fred

Estuary English, they call the speech now
sprawling round London. Fred Tarling
was an Essex farm-boy when that meant
he didn't go much further than a bus
would take him, if he had the fare.
His voice never fully lost the flavour
of country vowels.

He came from Buggers' 'ill, as he
insisted, to amuse his London family,
that Buckhurst Hill was called.
'Hallo, Taaalen', his friends would say,
according to the perhaps not strictly
truthful Fred, 'Got 'aaapenny?
We could 'ave aaalf a point'.

Fred spent time at the Front
in two wars: he left Essex to fight
the Boers under a blazing African
sun; in France, in the trenches,
he got frostbite. Fred had only two
anecdotes of war: one of the coffee
the French make from old socks,
and one of rubbing horse-dung
into an officer's new leather belt.

Uncle Fred had no language at all
to say how he felt.

A Child of The Thirties

wept
when Bud Flanagan sang
'pavement is my pillow';
she knew it was sad
that men slept there
but not
why they had to.

By her pillow
on lucky Sundays she found
a gold-wrapped chocolate.
She had a Dad with a job
to cycle to on Monday
a payday on Saturday.

Tucked up safe
in terraced comfort
she did not see
the desperation
at the dock gates
did not hear the feet
as Blackshirts marched
the streets of Whitechapel.

Songs on the wireless
taught her tears
before the world
taught her reasons.

Steel-tipped Boots

The pavement rang sharp and clear
at each clip-clop of steel-tipped boots.
Little spurts of sparks flew; sound
of steel, flash of fire, as men and boys
went to work that bent their backs.

'But *why* can't girls wear Blakeys?'
I asked my mother, sulky. If she had
responded with birthday boots I would
have danced along the singing streets
sparking my steel-capped joy.

Lizzie's Wars

Lizzie was not the prettiest
of the sisters, nor the smartest
not even the best-tempered;
still, there were young men
ready to offer a ring. One
by one she waved them goodbye
as they left for the trenches.

Lizzie was never a favourite;
still, she was one of the family
so they rented a shop where
she watched children scamper
back to their mothers with goods
she let them have on credit
'just till Friday'.

Lizzie was not the brightest
of the bunch; still, she jogged on
until another war came with its
regulations and ration-books and
it was all too much to cope with.

No use trawling through casualty-lists
looking for all those Lizzies.

Child on a Swing

Kicking careless feet
into the sky
between the window
and the washing
singing
my backyard freedom
on the swing

      a kick and thrust upwards
      a swoop down and up
      then a pause
      poised in equilibrium
      before the swoop down
      time held steady
      through years of summer

no past
no plans
timeless idling
hanging head downwards
happily dangling
going nowhere

      a slab of wood
      two bits of rope
      two hooks rammed on a pole
      a gift
      from a clumsy man
      to send his daughter
            swinging
                into memory.

Blitz

Suburb and City

1940

Londoners lived, it was often thought,
in a city, busy seat of government
of big banks, big business,
a rushing city of fine houses
tall churches everyone had heard of.

But these Londoners lived in a world
of work, of days spent making things
everyone had a use for—soap
telephones hairbrushes marmalade—
and the stuff of war.

So night after night destruction
in the dark; the lucky lost their homes
not their loved ones. Yet for some
the worst of all was the night
the bombs fell, but not near them.

Crouched below ground, guts
clenched, wave after relentless wave
of throbbing planes seemed to pass,
engines pulsing with slow menace
just above their throbbing heads.

'It's some other poor devils
getting it tonight' they said
crawling out of their shelters
with the dawn, having seen
the sky grow red at midnight.

That night historic London toppled
and burned around St Paul's. Hope
revived with the morning papers—
pictures of the dome still rearing
upwards into the sky.

Shelter

Too young to understand risk
but feeling fear her stomach churned
more at the unrelenting pulse
of planes than the shock of bombs.

Above ground London burned.
She watched the woodlice
poised above her bed ready
to curl into a ball and drop.

The shops the streets the houses turned
to rubble. She watched her mother
knit, one plain, one purl, making
that old familiar click.

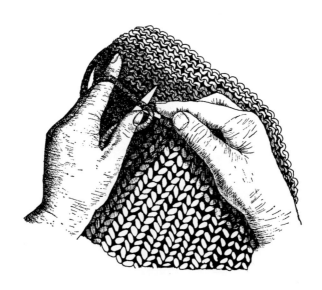

Wolfboy

Happily holding two jarring
thoughts in mind, I knew
the boy in my class was a boy
yet clearly he was a wolf:

the slink, the prowl, the grin,
the long dark head;
above all the eyes
that shifted and slid.

He couldn't read; he didn't
play or pinch the girls;
an unsettling presence;
he was sent to sit by me.

I was to help him read.
His grin stayed fixed, his eyes
flickered and hid. Could
Wolfboy share my unease?

After school he would search
war-damaged streets for shrapnel,
twisted bits of metal, useless scraps
littering bomb-sites.

Wolfboy found a car, abandoned.
He dropped a match in the tank.

Some mother, one teatime,
opened her door and heard that.

Addison and Steele in Plaistow, E13

Passmore Edwards built libraries for the poor.
Plaistow prospered a little since his and
Queen Victoria's day: a place where
respectable houses stood in row after dull row
until the war came. Then rosebay willowherb
grew in the gaps where houses had been.

I day-dreamed my way through school,
drifted through bomb-shattered streets
to the Passmore Edwards Library,
not in search of knowledge or progress,
but to let the world of books close round me
full of hidden comforts.

There, on a shelf marked 'essays and humour',
I found wit and restraint and elegance,
I found precision in language;
I found Addison and Steele.
The world they lived in was, you might say,
a closed book to me, and stayed so.

The two grey-wigged essayists
and the Victorian philanthropist
were journalists, writing for their day;
yet, across the years and the classes
they sent a spark of love for language
to smoulder in the imagination
of a child adrift in the London blitz.

Evacuees

Temperate English rain
falls on comfortable hills—
the Cotswolds.

London children
sent there to spend
war years in safety
among fresh green fields
by fresh clear streams
fretted for the familiar,
lost without mothers.

One by one
the little creatures flowed
back downstream
to the polluted air
to the polluted water
of Canning Town
Tidal Basin
Custom House,
heading home.

Sand

My bricks and mortar fog and foghorn
childhood was severed into two distinct
bucketsful of memory:

a bucket and spade on an infinite beach
once a year in that endless stretch
between one Christmas and the next;

then

everywhere every day red buckets,
fire-watchers' fag-ends in dirty sand,
ready for the next night's conflagrations.

The East End, 1940

The Kellys called their chickens
Gert and Dais; cramped
in the backyard coop
Gert and Dais soon sickened
and died.

The Kellys kept on
digging for victory
in the little plot
attacked by shrapnel
soot and the sulphurous
fog from factories.

Land not even a memory
they worked
their few square yards,
grew tomatoes
on earth piled over
the air-raid shelter.

No chance lost to cherish
that small green spot
in the heart.

A Sheltered Child

'You won't want to go to the funeral'
my mother told me, and turned away.
I spent the day with neighbours.

I didn't see the black cars come,
my pink-loving mother in black silk,
straight-backed, silent. I didn't see

his comrades from two wars,
black-banded, straight-backed,
form a shocked guard of honour.

I went back to school, carrying
a black ball of grief I had not
been shown how to handle.

After the War

When the war's over
said lovers with one last kiss at the station;
when the war's over
said the lonely, longing for letters;
when the war's over
said shoppers shivering in a line;
when the war's over
said women doubtfully fingering whalemeat.

After the war
said politicians, promising, promising.
After the war promised mothers
when Daddy comes home;
and there'll be picnics and peaches
and chocolate every day
said the children,
believing every word.

Five Victorian Vignettes

remembering the social reformers
and the anonymous poor

All the street-names and the words in italics in
'In Bethnal Green' and 'Hector Gavin' come from
*Sanitary Ramblings: being sketches and illustrations
of Bethnal Green* by Hector Gavin (1848).

In Bethnal Green

Once in rural Bethnal Green
streets were named *Swan Court*
Paradise Row Pleasant Place.
But the years brought squalor
and the poor were blamed
though now there was a factory
in *Hollybush Gardens.*

Hope of work drew
dairymaids from Wales
drew the Irish from their
green and dying land
to share the fogs and fevers
of London streets.

Once Bethnal Green was
a refuge for Huguenots
but now statistics showed
there was no more need
for hand-loom weavers.

Hector Gavin

Dr Hector Gavin put on his hat
his coat and sturdy boots to walk
through *Prospect Place* and
Sweet Apple Court where
listless children lived.

*Eight houses one privy one tap one
dustbin* he wrote in *Garden Place,
Hope Town.*   On he strode
through stinking streets where
families crowded in *shacks
like dog-kennels*
in his pursuit of proof.

Visiting the Weavers

To show they had souls
they came in silks and ribbons
in their carriages
(only the bold walked)
to view the recipients
of their Sunday charity.
Did any venture as far as
the common gardens?

On Sundays weavers
left their looms, some
to sing out their yearnings
in church or chapel
some straight to the plot,
the workless hungry
others weary with endless
streams of flashing silk.

Now they worked again in
precise shining patterns
but on Sundays
with living plants.
Doctor Gavin recorded
marvelling
the beauty they coaxed
from this sour earth.

Flying the Flag

Doctor Gavin fought cholera
throughout the Empire.
Killed in war by a random shot,
he lies beside soldiers
in a spot at Balaclava.

Not a glorious war
but England soon blazed
with imperial pride
waving flags
bellowing martial songs
to communal cheers
in music halls
called The Empire.

One way to get volunteers
to fight the battles.

Two Women

Marie Lloyd & Laura Ormiston Chant

Everybody loved Marie.
Marie was fun unlike
Mrs Ormiston Chant.
She was the prude
bent on closing the halls.
Or so the story went.

While Marie made money
with saucy songs
Laura nursed the sick
kept busy lecturing writing.
No feud between them in truth
but it made news.

Laura fought against
wrongs done to women
done to the poor. She saw
young girls procured
groomed and paraded
at The Empire.

Two strong women
Laura who poured
words from the heart
forgotten
outdated
Marie a presence long gone
still recalled
still celebrated.

In the Forest

Six Views of Refuge and Escape

Loughton Camp

Iron Age hill-fort in Epping Forest of the Trinovantes about 55 BC. The fort was probably abandoned about the time of Caesar's first invasion.

From this ridge cleared of trees we can look out
to see our cattle, our fields of barley, watch for
traders returning from unimaginable distances,
look for spies, marauders, armies. We are strong,
the strongest. There are rumours—the women
are uneasy—but we are invincible. Surely.

John Clare

A patient in Dr Allen's asylum at High Beech in Epping Forest from 1837 until 1841 when he escaped to walk to his home near Peterborough.

He settled under a hornbeam
to light his pipe and watch the squirrels
feeling the majestic forest quiver with life.
But it was not home.

Back there in the cottage
he clustered with the family
then was off out windswept
in the open vistas
of his own territory.
He knew that land
thistle by rush by lady-smock.

Why did Patty not come
to take him home?
He sank back into his mind

to find Patty. Patty and Mary
and Byron. Sometimes he forgot
other people couldn't see them,
more real than anyone here,
though there were pretty girls
in the forest.

In the morning he packed his pipe
and tobacco put some books
in his pockets and struck out north.

Home.

Alfred Tennyson

Tennyson lived near Matthew Allen's asylum 1837-1840;
he began writing In Memoriam *at that time. It includes*
the lines: 'Nature red in tooth and claw'.

Grieving for his lost friend
oppressed by bad reviews
and lack of money
he sought solace
in Dr Allen's asylum
among the healing trees.

He stumbled through undergrowth
saw life creeping through the forest
twisting the roots, bending the branches
sensed the vigour of earthworms pushing
pushing thick earth up to the light
but found nothing to animate
the black blood of the Tennysons.

Hallam had helped but
Hallam was dead and hope
was long ago.
Long, long ago.

A blackbird pulled a worm from the earth
stretching and swallowing it with practised
moves and a bright eye. He remembered
a game-keeper in Lincolnshire moving
with confident step, swinging a rabbit
mangled by a trap from a capable hand.
Death; death and ravine and gore.

No t quite a patient
almost a friend,
he retreated to the comfort
of Dr Allen's drawing room.

Edward Thomas

*Posted with the Artists Rifles to Suntrap Camp, High Beech
in Epping Forest July 1915, approximately on the site of
Loughton Camp*

Living in a leaky hut
the food foul, no solitude
nor time to write

still he had escaped
for a while
from money worries

from wrangling at home
from guilt
from decisions

and he was growing
to love Essex
the land, the names.

He hid a notebook
under a magazine
and began to write

his legacy
to his elder daughter.
What had he got to leave

but language?

Ivor Gurney

Posted to Wintry Camp, Epping Forest June 1915 with
2nd/5th Gloucestershire Regiment

June, on May Hill. June, even here
in Essex. And here he was stuck
in Wintry Camp. Wintry Camp!
And confined to barracks again too.
He must remember to clean that rifle.

But it wasn't so bad in camp
with the Glosters, their voices
scented with the Severn.
And all the exercise
was doing him good
whereas the food wasn't.

Still, he could make a joke of it
when he wrote to his friends.
At the thought of friends
he stood again looking across
at the Malvern Hills in summer.

Gloucester

where he belonged.

Connaught Water

1920s. West Ham is adjacent to the forest.

Safe now from shell-burst and boredom of the trench
children chasing dogs into Connaught Water then
the dogs kicking dirt into the sandwiches
laughing because the sun was shining
on a Bank Holiday and surely
surely there could never
be another war after that last one and
surely their jobs were safe and the homes
they were making for their families would
        stay
            safe?